People of
Michigan

Marcia Schonberg

Heinemann Library
Chicago, Illinois

Designed by Heinemann Library
Maps by Kimberly Saar/Heinemann Library
Photo research by Jill Birschbach and Kathy Creech
Printed in the United States by Lake Book
   Manufacturing, Inc.

08 07 06 05 04
10 9 8 7 6 5 4 3 2 1

**Library of Congress
Cataloging-in-Publication Data**
Schonberg, Marcia.
  People of Michigan / by Marcia Schonberg.
     v. cm. -- (Heinemann state studies)
Includes bibliographical references and index.
Contents: Michigan's people -- Michigan's earliest residents -- Early French explorers and missionaries in Michigan -- Settlers come to Michigan -- Cultural groups in Michigan -- Contributors to Michigan's growth -- Michigan people and the auto industry -- Michigan achievers.
   ISBN 1-4034-0661-8 -- ISBN 1-4034-2680-5 (pbk.) 1. Ethnology--Michigan--Juvenile literature. 2. Minorities--Michigan--Juvenile literature. 3. Immigrants--Michigan--Juvenile literature. 4. Michigan--Population--Juvenile literature. 5. Michigan--History--Juvenile literature. 6. Michigan--Biography--Juvenile literature. [1. Michigan--Population. 2. Ethnology--Michigan. 3. Minorities--Michigan. 4. Immigrants--Michigan. 5. Michigan--Biography.] I. Title. II. Series.
   F575.A1S36 2003
   977.4--dc22   2003012285

Acknowledgments
The author and publishers are grateful to the following for permission to reproduce copyright material:
Title page (L-R) Bettmann/Corbis, Reuters NewMedia Inc./Corbis, Bettmann/Corbis; contents page (L-R) Rufus R. Folkks/Corbis, Ed Kashi/Corbis, Stapleton Collection/Corbis; pp. 4, 30, 35, 36, 39b, 40b, 42 Bettmann/Corbis; p. 8 Ohio Historical Society; p. 10 Henry F. Zeman; p. 12 Jim Allor Photography; p. 13 Corbis; pp. 14, 29, 31, 32 Burton Historical Collection/Detroit Public Library; p. 15 Stapleton Collection/Corbis; pp. 16, 27 State Archives of Michigan; p. 17 Muskegon County Museum; p. 18 Ed Kashi/Corbis; p. 19 Hope College Archives; p. 20 Robert Lifson/Heinemann Library; pp. 21, 22 Dennis Cox/WorldViews; p. 23 Courtesy of Cleary University; p. 24 Phil Schemeister/Corbis; p. 25 James L. Amos/Corbis; p. 26 The Detroit News Archives; p. 28 Bob Krist/Corbis; pp. 33t, 40t Hulton-Deutsch Collection/Corbis; p. 33b Wally McNamee/Corbis; p. 34 AFP/Corbis; p. 37 Roger Rossmeyer/Corbis; p. 38t Rufus R. Folkks/Corbis; p. 38b Bill Sikes/AP Wide World; p. 39t Courtesy of W. K. Kellogg Foundation; p. 41 Douglas C. Pizac/AP Wide World Photos; p. 44t Reuters NewMedia Inc./Corbis; p. 44b Matthew Mendelsohn/Corbis

Cover photographs by (top, L-R) Matthew Mendelsohn/Corbis, Bettmann/Corbis, Kevin Fleming/Corbis, Roger Rossmeyer/Corbis; (main) Corbis

The publisher would like to thank expert reader Francis X. Blouin Jr., director of the Bentley Historical Society in Ann Arbor.

Also, special thanks to Alexandra Fix and Bernice Anne Houseward for their curriculum guidance.

Some words are shown in bold, **like this.** You can find out what they mean by looking in the glossary.

Contents

Michigan's People

The people of Michigan have several nicknames. Some refer to themselves as Michiganians. Others prefer to be called Michiganders. People living in the Upper Peninsula are often proud to be called "Yoopers." No matter what nickname a person from Michigan prefers, the residents of the state are what make it a great place to live and visit.

WHO ARE THE PEOPLE OF MICHIGAN?

Michigan's people have many **cultural** backgrounds. They have come to the state from all over the country and the world. Some families can trace their **heritage** back to the people who settled the state, while others are newcomers who **migrated** here for the many opportunities Michigan offers.

More than 130 **ethnic** groups are represented in Michigan. Some of these groups include Dutch, Finnish, Polish, Italians, Swedes, French Canadians, Asians, Germans, and Romanians.

MICHIGAN'S CENSUS DATA

Michigan is ranked as the eighth-largest state in the United States. As of 2001, Michigan was home to more

This girl is dressed in a traditional Dutch outfit.

than 9,990,000 residents. Wayne County, which includes the city of Detroit, is the eleventh-largest county in the United States, with over two million residents.

Michigan's people represent many races and ethnicities. Eighty percent are Caucasian and 14 percent are African American. This means that out of every 100 people in Michigan, 80 of them are Caucasian and 14 are African American. Other peoples, such as Asians, Hispanics, and Native Americans, make up a very small percentage of the population. When added all together, these groups of people total less than seven percent of the people living in Michigan.

WHERE DO MICHIGAN'S PEOPLE LIVE?

Michigan has a lot of space in which its residents can live. According to the 2000 U.S. Census, almost 318,000 people lived in the Upper Peninsula. The Lower Peninsula holds many more people, but they are also spread out over a large space. Detroit is home to almost one million people. Detroit is much larger than

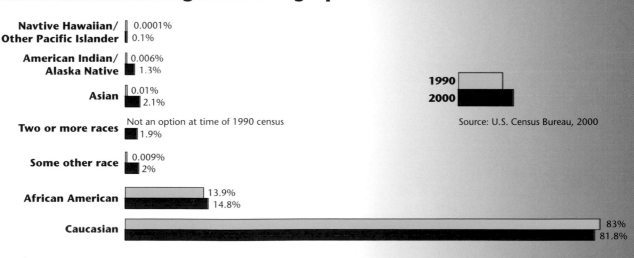

Michigan's Demographics: 1990 vs. 2000

	1990	2000
Navtive Hawaiian/ Other Pacific Islander	0.0001%	0.1%
American Indian/ Alaska Native	0.006%	1.3%
Asian	0.01%	2.1%
Two or more races	Not an option at time of 1990 census	1.9%
Some other race	0.009%	2%
African American	13.9%	14.8%
Caucasian	83%	81.8%

Source: U.S. Census Bureau, 2000

*Michigan's population became more **diverse** between 1990 and 2000.*

Grand Rapids, the second-largest city, which has nearly 200,000 people. Eight of the ten largest cities in Michigan are located in the eastern part of the Lower Peninsula.

During the 1990s, population growth was the fastest in areas near big cities that once were **rural.** For example, areas such as Livingston, Washtenaw, Ottawa, and Kent counties experienced a huge growth in population, especially of families with young children.

Detroit has the most people of all the cities in Michigan. It has over ten times the number of people in Westland, Michigan's tenth-largest city.

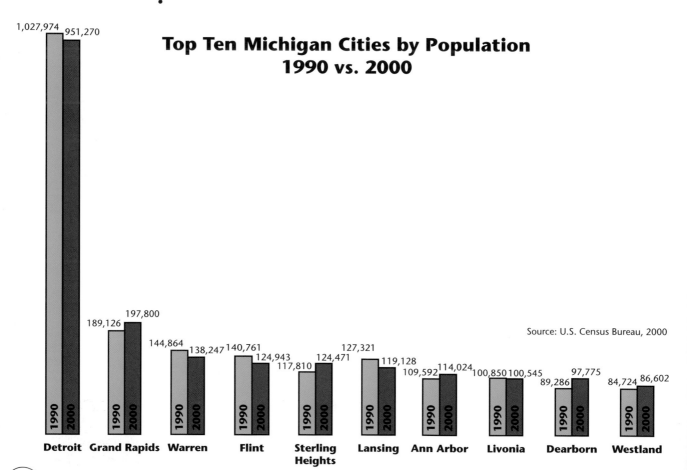

Top Ten Michigan Cities by Population 1990 vs. 2000

Source: U.S. Census Bureau, 2000

City	1990	2000
Detroit	1,027,974	951,270
Grand Rapids	189,126	197,800
Warren	144,864	138,247
Flint	140,761	124,943
Sterling Heights	117,810	124,471
Lansing	127,321	119,128
Ann Arbor	109,592	114,024
Livonia	100,850	100,545
Dearborn	89,286	97,775
Westland	84,724	86,602

Michigan's Population Change by County, 1990 vs. 2000

Population Change
- Population gain
- Population loss

Almost all of Michigan's counties gained residents between 1990 and 2000.

Population trends in Michigan reflect changes in society. Employment opportunities allow people to leave big cities like Detroit and move to **suburban** areas. People with families sometimes prefer to live in suburban areas because the school districts are often better than in other areas. Some older Michiganders choose to retire "up north" to the Upper Peninsula. Technology also makes it possible for people to live far away from their jobs and **telecommute.**

No matter where they live, many people of Michigan have made great contributions to both the state and the country. The state of Michigan is proud to claim these people as its own.

Michigan's First Residents

Michigan's earliest peoples arrived about 15,000 years ago, during **prehistoric** times. These early peoples roamed across North America as they hunted. The animals they hunted, such as the **mammoth** and **mastodon,** were **migrating** to new places. These hunters followed prehistoric animals across the Bering Strait when it was a land bridge connecting Asia with North America.

PALEO-INDIANS

Large animals provided food, clothing, and shelter for the Paleo-Indians, the name scientists gave to this ancient group. The Paleo-Indians were nomads, people who roam and do not live in one place. Animal bones and arrow points found by **archaeologists** suggest that the Paleo-Indians reached the eastern part of the Lower Peninsula of Michigan. When they reached the area now known as Flint, they made hunting weapons and tools from the flint they found. Paleo-Indians used animal fur for clothing, hides for tents, and meat for food.

Paleo-Indians used flint to make various tools, including knives, scrapers, and points to throw like spears.

OLD COPPER INDIANS

Archaeologists do not know what the next group of ancient people in Michigan called themselves. These people had no written language. Scientists sometimes had to make up

When the first people came to the Americas, the climate was much colder than it is today. Much of the land was covered in glaciers. People had to find areas to live where the climate was warmer, such as the area that later became known as Michigan.

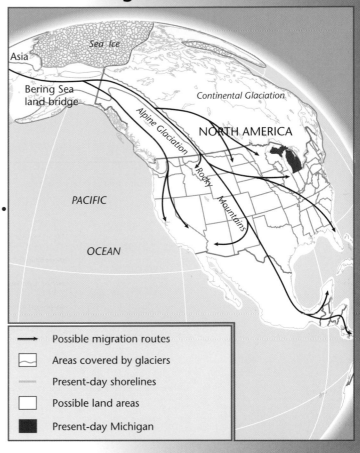

names to identify prehistoric people. They called the people who mined copper near the Keewanau Peninsula the Old Copper Indians. This group discovered nearly pure copper close to the earth's surface. They used it to cover the edges of their weapons and to make ceremonial objects. They also traded copper with tribes in other parts of the country.

WOODLAND CULTURE

The next group to settle in Michigan was the Woodland **culture.** This group was also named by archaeologists. The Woodland tribes were not nomads like the tribes before them. The Woodland people created communities. They farmed as their main source of food. They planted the "Three Sisters"—corn, beans, and squash—together in little dirt hills.

The Woodland people were also known as mound-builders because of the mounds of earth they built as a place for worship and burial. In Michigan, they left behind about 1,000 burial mounds, located near the Grand and Muskegon rivers. Like tribes before and after them, they settled close to rivers and lakes. They used the waterways for transportation, and the rivers and lakes provided food.

THREE FIRES

The "Three Fires" tribes settled in different regions of Michigan and had different practices, but they considered themselves a family. They spoke a similar language. The tribes in this family were the Potawatomi, Ottawa, and Ojibway.

The Ottawa lived along Lake Michigan on the western coast of the Lower Peninsula. The Ojibway, called "Chippewa" by the Ottawa, lived in the Upper Peninsula and on the eastern part of the Lower Peninsula. The Potowatomi tribe moved east across the state, away from Lake Michigan.

The Norton Mound Group, built by the moundbuilders, is located in Grand Rapids. There were once over 30 mounds in the area, but only 11 remain today.

NATIVE AMERICANS IN MICHIGAN TODAY

Today, Michigan is home to about 58,000 Native Americans. There are 12 federally recognized tribes in Michigan. Thousands of native peoples live on reservations, but many more live in communities throughout Michigan. Michigan's Native Americans work at many **occupations,** just like other residents. Some Native Americans prefer the work of their ancestors, such as hunting and fishing. Others operate or work in casinos on their reservations. There are 17 gambling casinos in Michigan run by Native American groups. Michigan's Native Americans continue to have an influence on the state and maintain their **cultural** beliefs through celebrations, powwows, and other gatherings.

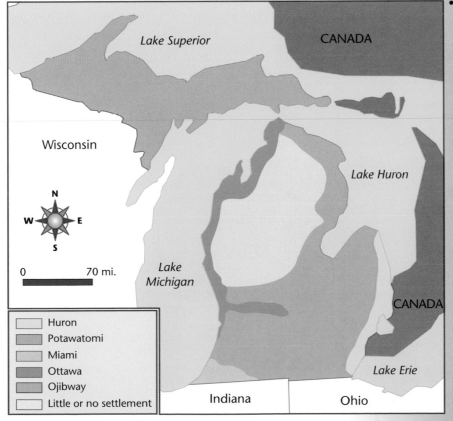

Tribes of Michigan

Lake Superior

CANADA

Wisconsin

Lake Huron

N
W   E
S

0   70 mi.

Lake Michigan

CANADA

Lake Erie

Indiana   Ohio

Huron
Potawatomi
Miami
Ottawa
Ojibway
Little or no settlement

This map shows the general area where the tribes of Michigan lived. Native Americans often moved when hunting for food, and they did not follow strict borderlines.

Early French Explorers and Missionaries in Michigan

The waters around Michigan brought many explorers to the area who were trying to find shortcuts to Asia. An explorer and **Jesuit** priest, Pierre Francois Xavier de Charlevoix, was one of them. The city of Charlevoix, located on Lake Michigan near the top of the Lower Peninsula, was named for this French explorer.

Father Jacques Marquette built a **mission** at Sault Ste. Marie in 1671. This is the oldest missionary settlement in Michigan and the Midwest. Today, a city, county, and river are all named in honor of Father Marquette.

Charlevoix's waters now are used by pleasure boaters and people who enjoy the beautiful scenery.

René Robert Cavalier, Sieur de La Salle, a French explorer who discovered rivers and land throughout the Midwest, built the first **fort** in the Lower Peninsula in 1696. He called it Fort Miami, after the Miami River that ran past the fort. Both the fort and the river were named for a Native American tribe, the Miami, who lived in the region. Later, the names of both the fort and the river were changed to St. Joseph.

Fort Michilimackinac was built on the **strait** of St. Ignace in the Upper Peninsula. A trading post was established here in 1673, and it became a military fort in 1715. The fort served as a supply post for French traders operating in the western Great Lakes region.

René Robert Cavalier, Sieur de La Salle

One of this fort's early commanders was Antoine de la Mothe Cadillac. After several years, he convinced the king of France to allow him to build another fort in the Lower Peninsula. Cadillac dreamed of building a permanent fort big enough for settlers and soldiers. His fort along the Detroit River was called Fort Pontchartrain du De Troit. The first part of the name honored King Louis XIV's officer, Count Pontchartrain, who helped Cadillac convince the king to add a new fort. The ending, De Troit, means "the strait" in French. However, Cadillac's plan and the founding of Detroit on July 24, 1701, did not attract many settlers. Most eastern pioneers thought it was too dangerous to travel north into the lands that would become Michigan. French settlers in New France, or Canada as it is now called, felt the same.

*This is an artist's drawing of the original **Fort** Pontchartrain. Today, the Pontchartrain Hotel stands in this spot in Detroit.*

In 1754 war broke out between the British and the French and Native American **allies.** It was called the French and Indian War. The groups were battling over control of the upper Ohio River valley, which included the area which is now Michigan. The defeat of French troops in 1763 left the British in command of the area.

French Forts

The places where Michigan's French forts stood can still be visited today.

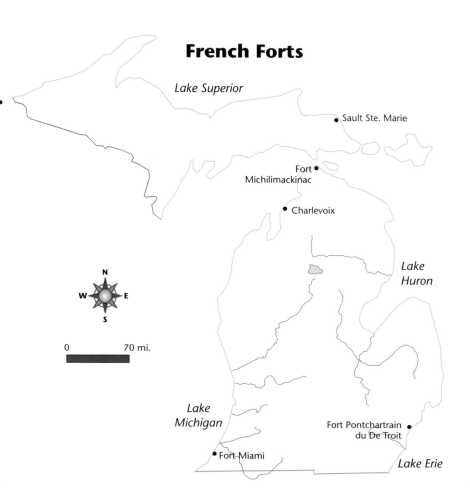

Lake Superior

Sault Ste. Marie

Fort Michilimackinac

Charlevoix

Lake Huron

N
W E
S

0   70 mi.

Lake Michigan

Fort Pontchartrain du De Troit

Fort Miami

Lake Erie

Settlers Come to Michigan

Michigan became a territory in 1805. Lewis Cass, governor of the Michigan Territory from 1813 to 1832, encouraged settlers to come to Michigan. Less than 5,000 people lived in Michigan when he began his work. Although it was difficult to bring settlers to the Michigan Territory, with Cass's help, the population grew to about 9,000 by 1820.

TRANSPORTATION ROUTES BRING SETTLERS

In 1825 the Erie Canal was completed in New York state and **canal** construction began in Ohio. Canal and steamboat transportation made reaching the Michigan Territory easier because roads at this time were no more than paths made by Native Americans. One of the famous Native American paths, the Sauk Trail, became the Chicago Road. Workers began creating the road in 1825. It took travelers across the state from Detroit to the western border of Lake Michigan. The I-94 highway follows the same path today. Roads similar to this one brought pioneers to Michigan. These roads also brought products to and from markets farther away. As more people chose to make the territory their home, area leaders began discussing statehood.

Lewis Cass

Michigan became the 26th state in the United States on January 26, 1837. Stevens T. Mason was elected as the new state's first governor.

All Aboard for Michigan

During the years following statehood, Michigan's population grew steadily. It was still not as easy to get to as other states. Railroads connected Michigan with other areas, but much of the land remained unsettled. Forests, dark with pine trees, were not as **fertile** as the land in other states, such as Illinois. Land was swampy. Farmers preferred to settle elsewhere, but as the forested land in Michigan was cleared, the soil was able to support farming. New settlers arrived to farm.

By the mid-1800s, workers, especially lumberjacks who heard of the thick pine forests, arrived from Europe and eastern states. Many others came from foreign countries.

This picture was taken at Barnes-Hecker mine in 1926. This mine was the site of the worst mining disaster in Michigan history. Fifty-one men, including some in this picture, were killed when the mine caved in.

Charles Hackley: Lumber Baron

Charles H. Hackley was one of many lumber **barons** who moved to Muskegon in 1856. With the wealth he earned in the lumber industry, he helped the community grow and succeed by building schools and libraries. He believed in the importance of education, especially in the trades. He began trade schools to help students learn an **occupation** that would help them earn a living. Hackley served on the local school board. He also believed in supporting the community, donating about $6,000,000 to the city of Muskegon.

They came from Great Britain, Ireland, and Scotland. Germans, Dutch, Norwegians, Finnish, French, and Belgians soon followed. Many **immigrants** who came from European countries were very poor. They looked for food and jobs in Michigan. Many wanted to farm but ended up taking jobs in mines, in the lumber **industry,** and on the railways because these jobs were more readily available.

LUMBERJACKS AND MINERS ARRIVE

The mining and lumber industries attracted immigrants who were not interested in farming. Norwegian, Finnish, and Swedish lumberjacks were used to life in the lumber camps and mill towns in their native countries of Norway, Finland, and Sweden. Many types of trees grew in Michigan, but it was the huge pine trees that became the favorite of lumberjacks. As eastern states such as Maine used up their lumber, workers moved to Michigan. By 1880, Michigan became the lumber center of the United States. It supplied the lumber to build new cities in the western states. Mill towns grew throughout Michigan. Some, such as Grand Rapids and Muskegon, are **prosperous** cities today. Others became ghost towns once the lumberjacks left.

Cultural Groups in Michigan

Michigan is home to people of all races and **ethnicities.** The 2000 census recorded 523,589 people living in Michigan who were born in other countries. That equals about one in five of all Michigan residents. The Census Bureau estimated in 2000 that there were about 1,298,000 people in Michigan who were either **immigrants** or children of immigrants. These people bring their **heritage,** traditions, and beliefs to Michigan, making it a diverse state.

Michigan also has the largest Arabian, Bulgarian, Croatian, and Romanian populations of the entire United States.

*Dutch immigrants brought their **cultural** values and religion to Michigan.*

DUTCH

The Dutch settled in several communities in Michigan. Holland, Grand Rapids, Zeeland, and Kalamazoo remain highly populated with people of Dutch **descent** today.

There were three main waves of immigration that brought the Dutch to the United States from the Netherlands. The first group came in 1845. These people, called Calvinists, were looking for religious freedom. The Netherlands were also suffering from potato **famines,** cattle **plagues,** low **agricultural** prices, high land prices, natural disasters, and **cholera.** A second wave of immigration to the U.S. occurred around 1880, when there was another agricultural crisis in the Netherlands and food was scarce. The last wave came after World War II (1939–1945). Much of the Netherlands had been destroyed by the fighting. The Dutch were afraid of nearby Germany's power and feared another war. They came to the U.S. to start new lives in safety.

De Zwaan is the only authentic Dutch windmill working in the United States today.

• •

One of the greatest contributions the Dutch made to Michigan reflects their strong belief in education. There are two colleges founded by the Dutch in western Michigan. Located in downtown Holland, Michigan, is Hope College and Western Theological Seminary. This private school has approximately 3,000 students. Calvin College is located in Grand Rapids and has approximately 4,000 students.

In 1997 Holland, Michigan, celebrated its **sesquicentennial.** In the 150 years since its founding, Holland's Dutch **heritage** is still evident all around. On Windmill Island is an **authentic** Dutch windmill called De Zwaan. De Zwaan once stood in the Netherlands, was taken apart, and brought to Windmill Island in Holland, where it was put back together in 1964. De Zwaan is around 250 years old and still grinds flour today.

Each May, the Tulip Time Festival is also held in Holland. More than 1,500 people participate in the festival. Downtown Holland hosts the Dutch Marktplaats, which has authentic Dutch food, crafts, music, and souvenirs. The festival starts with scrubbing the main street, and the people wear traditional wooden shoes. There are three parades during the week-long festival, which starts on the Wednesday closest to May 15. In addition, many musical events and historical tours occur during Tulip Time.

GERMANS

Germans make up the largest **ethnic** group in Michigan, representing over 2.6 million **descendants,** or 22 percent of Michigan's population. Yet, unlike other **immigrant** groups, Germans have not kept their language and **cultural** traditions as part of a distinct community as the

Dutch have. Today, only the villages of Frankenmuth and Gaylord reflect German communities that existed in both **rural** and **urban** Michigan.

The first Germans arrived in Michigan in the 1830s and 1840s, fleeing political problems in their homeland. German musicians, teachers, and professionals joined increasing numbers of immigrants in Detroit. By 1880 20 percent of the city's population was German-born. Most of these immigrants settled in an area known as Germantown. Many opened shops and businesses such as breweries and tailoring shops. Harmonie Park, its name associated with the nearby Harmonie Club, was an important center of Germantown. By the 1920s elegant clubhouses and buildings had become centers of German-American cultural life. Numerous German-American singing societies—some that started around the time of the Civil War (1861–1865)—had memberships in the thousands.

After World War II (1939–1945), the German-American community of Detroit worked with the Michigan Relief for Germans in Europe to provide clothing and food to war-torn Germany. As a result of this combined effort, the German-American Cultural Center (GACC) was founded in 1950 as a way to bring together many of the German-American organizations of the Detroit area.

Over three million people visit Frankenmuth every year. The town still has the feel of a small German village.

The German-American community continued to grow, and as many as 20,000 people would attend the annual German-American Folksfest in Detroit.

Today, more than 16 German companies are doing business and employing 60,000 workers in southeastern Michigan alone. There are 134 German-based companies in Oakland County and 27 in Washtenaw County. Daimler Chrysler is one of the well-known corporations with ties to Germany.

A Polish festival is held every Labor Day weekend in Hamtramck.

POLISH

More than 900,000 Polish people live in Michigan today. Polish people make up the largest group of **immigrants** in the state. Michigan ranks third in the country in its number of Polish residents.

Between 1795 and 1918, Poland did not exist as a country. It was during this time that many Poles immigrated to the United States. The peak year of Polish immigration was 1912, with more than 170,000 Poles arriving in the United States. Many went to live near cities such as Detroit and Chicago. They were looking for **industrial** jobs, especially in automobile factories.

Polish **heritage** is still present in Michigan today. The town of Bronson started Polish Festival Days in 1969. The festival features Polish foods, polka dances, Polish folk entertainment, and arts and crafts. A Polish **cultural** center, with **authentic** crafts and **artifacts,** is set up in the Bronson Community Center during the festival. Grand Rapids also hosts a Polish festival each year.

IRISH

The Potato **Famine** of 1845 was terrible for the people of Ireland. As a result, a wave of immigrants arrived in the United States, and many made their way to Michigan. Irish people were hard workers and often worked extremely long hours at very difficult jobs for very little pay. Even so, Irish immigrants saved what money they could and sent it to relatives in Ireland.

Several Irish immigrants made a positive impact on Michigan history. In 1883 Irish immigrant Patrick Roger Cleary founded Cleary's School of Penmanship. Starting with only two students, he soon attracted more by offering other business-related classes. In 1889 the school's name was changed to Cleary Business College. Thomas Hume was the business partner of Charles H. Hackley from 1881 to 1905. Hume came to Muskegon in 1872 and began working as Hackley's bookkeeper. After Hackley's death, Hume was a leader in transforming Muskegon from a lumber town to a major manufacturing center.

Cleary University serves 1,100 students studying business-related fields today.

The Irish culture is still evident in Michigan today. For example, Wexford County was named after a county in Ireland and populated by Irish immigrants. Clare County was named by Irish settlers homesick for County Clare in Ireland. There are also numerous Irish heritage festivals held around the state each year.

Contributors to Michigan's Growth

Farming, mining, and lumbering opportunities attracted newcomers to Michigan. In 1855 the first **locks** at the Soo Canal at Sault Ste. Marie opened. The locks equalized the water levels between Lake Huron and Lake Superior so **schooners** and freighters could easily travel from one Great Lake to another. This allowed **industries** in the area to ship materials on Lakes Erie, Ontario, and Huron.

The Soo Locks is the largest waterway traffic system on Earth.

A worker at the Herman Miller Furniture Company in Zeeland saws a wooden desktop.

FURNITURE CITY

Businesses related to the lumber industry contributed to Michigan's early growth. Settlers included cabinetmakers who were eager to use the native woods. Some of their shops grew to be large furniture companies. With nearly 200 furniture manufacturers, Grand Rapids became known as Furniture City and was the furniture capital of the United States. Cabinetmaker William Haldane was the first of many furniture craftspeople in Grand Rapids. Many other cabinetmakers followed him. Julius Berkey and George Gay created quality furniture at their company, Berkey and Gay. Some companies created

The Dry Kiln

A. D. Linn and Z. Clark Thwing solved a problem all cabinetmakers shared. Lumber needs be very dry before it can be used for building, but it could take several years to dry lumber. Linn and Thwing developed a drying machine, called the dry kiln, to speed up the process. This invention allowed companies to specialize in creating certain types of furniture such as matching bedroom suites or office furniture.

highly decorated, fancy pieces while others made functional furniture for offices and schools. Today, Grand Rapids is still home to headquarters and factories for several furniture companies, including Steelcase, Incorporated; Haworth; Herman Miller; and American Seating Company.

CHEMICAL INDUSTRY

Michigan also had an **industry** born from another one of Michigan's natural resources: chemicals. One of Michigan's major natural resources—salt mines—led researchers and inventors to move to Michigan and build companies that are still important today. Much of the Lower Peninsula sits on huge salt deposits that were

There is a city beneath a city 1,200 feet below the ground in Detroit. Equipment similar to what you might see at a construction site above ground works to mine salt underground.

Hervey Parke (left) and George Davis (right) founded Parke-Davis and Company in a small drugstore in Detroit on October 26, 1866.

formed millions of years ago. Salt is still heavily mined under Detroit, where the salt beds are close to the surface. Herbert H. Dow, an Ohio-based chemist, began removing other chemicals from salt dissolved in water. The Dow Chemical Corporation, founded in Midland in 1897, created more than 400 chemicals from salt.

From these chemical resources came another industry in Michigan. Medicines prescribed by doctors to treat specific illnesses got their start in companies based in Detroit. Dr. Samuel Duffield opened a drugstore in 1862 and went into business with Hervey Parke and George Davis. That was the beginning of a partnership called Parke-Davis. It became the largest company of its type in the world before 1900. Similarly, Dr. William E. Upjohn began a company in Kalamazoo that produced easy-to-swallow pills. The pills he produced dissolved after they were swallowed, allowing the medicine to work.

Michigan People and the Auto Industry

Michigan has always provided good jobs in different areas of the manufacturing **industry.** But the early founders of Michigan's auto industry did more than create jobs for autoworkers. They changed manufacturing methods throughout the United States and the world.

The city of Lansing is the car capital of North America, producing nearly 500,000 Pontiacs, Oldsmobiles, Chevrolets, and Cadillacs every year.

William C. Durant (1861–1947) was the founder of General Motors, in Flint. He and his business partner, Josiah Dallas Dort, operated the largest carriage manufacturing company in the United States during the 1890s. After the first cars, called horseless carriages, were developed in Michigan by Henry Ford in 1896, Durant began to think about auto manufacturing, too. It was his idea to build many different models of cars. He began by buying the Oldsmobile line from Ransom Olds before adding the Buick Company. Durant's company also bought the Oakland Automobile Company in 1909, which later became Pontiac. Then he paid $4.5 million for the rights to Cadillac. Some of the companies Durant purchased did not last long, but General Motors still manufactures many of the auto brands that began in the early 1900s.

William C. Durant

Ransom E. Olds (1864–1950) was building gasoline engines in his Lansing factory before 1900. He had the idea of building an affordable gasoline-powered car that would meet the needs of most people. Olds opened his own engine shop in 1890. He then opened his REO Motor Car Company in 1904. The company name came from the initials in his name, and it produced 6,500 autos by 1905. Olds is called the "father of the automobile industry" because he opened the first automobile factory in Michigan.

Ransom E. Olds

Henry Ford's vehicles changed the lives of people everywhere. Travel became much easier, and the cars could be used for many purposes, including hauling lumber and farm products.

Henry Ford (1863–1947) built the first affordable car, the Model T, in 1908. He had been building cars since 1896, when he first tested his **quadricycle.** A man named Charles King actually drove the first gasoline powered auto in Michigan—three months before Henry Ford introduced his car. Although neither man was the inventor of the first automobile, Henry Ford often receives the credit.

Henry Ford was a smart businessperson who was not afraid to take chances. His Model T became so popular that he could not keep up with demand by building one car at a time. He added an assembly line to speed up production in his auto factory. He also used **interchangeable** parts to reduce production costs. A conveyer belt moved automatically past a production line of factory workers. Each person had one job to do as the product moved along the moving belt. This process, called the division of labor, became the way future manufacturers would operate. Ford's new idea saved time and money. By using the conveyer belt, he lowered the price of his car, from about $850 each to $290 and sold one million cars in 1915 alone. Unlike William Durant, Henry Ford's idea was to build many cars of the same model and the same color. This kept the cost of the cars low. Ford built his black Model T until 1927.

In 1936 Henry Ford started the Ford Foundation. It is an organization that develops and supports hundreds of educational, **humanitarian,** and research projects around the world. It is one of the largest charity foundations in the United States.

John Dodge

John Dodge (1864–1920) and **Horace Dodge** (1868–1920) were born in Niles. They began their inventive careers by building bicycles. As the auto **industry** grew, they began building parts for cars. Their company, called the Dodge Brothers, created the axles, engines, and transmissions for Oldsmobiles and Fords. In 1914 they used their wealth to build their own auto plant in Hamtramck, near Detroit. They were early producers of cars with an all-steel body and baked-on paint finishes. Their cars were known for their dependability. In fact, historians say that the word *dependability* did not exist before the Dodge Brothers used it in advertising. Their Dodge cars and trucks were used in World War I (1914–1918). After their deaths, the Dodge brothers' company was purchased by the Chrysler Corporation.

Horace Dodge

David Dunbar Buick (1854–1929) came to Michigan as a toddler. He was born in Scotland but grew up in Detroit. His father owned a plumbing company, and Buick worked in the plumbing industry as a teenager.

David Buick

He invented the process of covering iron bathtubs with a white coating called porcelain. The white bathtubs were very popular. Buick also invented other plumbing devices, but he became fascinated with engines and automobiles and moved on to creating engines and auto parts. He began manufacturing Buick automobiles in 1902. He borrowed money to start his company and within a few years, he joined what would later become General Motors. Disagreements led him to leave the auto **industry** and, unlike other automobile **barons,** Buick died poor.

AUTO MAKING IN THE 1900S

Auto manufacturing gave Michigan's population a boost in the early 1900s. Workers moved from other states and other countries for high-paying jobs in Michigan's factories. If workers did not know how to speak English, they attended schools set up by Henry Ford. They produced equipment during World War I (1914–1918). However, the **Great Depression** caused workers to lose their jobs, especially automakers. People could not afford new cars.

Michigan residents recovered during World War II (1939–1945). Auto manufacturers stopped producing cars and began producing only wartime vehicles such as tanks, jeeps, ships, bombers, and airplanes. Women took the factory jobs that belonged to men before the United States entered World War II. Because they worked in factories for the first time, women on the assembly lines were nicknamed "Rosie the Riveter."

When soldiers returned home, they were eager to buy new cars and homes for their families. The auto and construction industries boomed again. Travel led to other jobs and industries. With more people traveling by car, roadside restaurants, and motels were needed.

Lee Iacocca (b. 1924) began working for the Ford Motor Company in 1946 as an engineering trainee. He introduced Ford's famous Mustang in 1964. Less than 25 years after he began working for Ford, he became president of the Ford Motor Company. He was an **ambitious** person who was not afraid to speak up. Those qualities both helped and hurt Iacocca. He lost his job at Ford after an argument with Henry Ford II in 1978. Iacocca took over as president of Chrysler Corporation later that year at the lowest point in Chrysler history. He saved the company by getting a huge loan from the federal government. The creation of the Chrysler minivan gave the company another boost, and Lee Iacocca became the highest-paid executive in the United States.

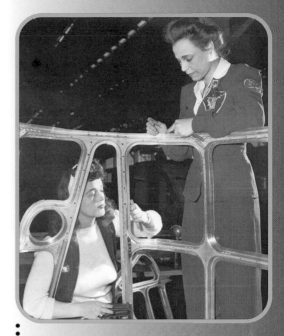

These women are inspecting the frame of a B-24 bomber at the Ford Willow Run factory.

Lee Iacocca

Michigan Achievers

Many Michiganders have taken risks, making changes in Michigan and across the globe. Some of their ideas led to discoveries that are part of our lives even today. Other people from Michigan became famous artists, athletes, writers, and entertainers.

Aardema, Verna (b. 1911), author. Aardema was born in New Era, Michigan. She is the author of the Caldecott-winning picture book, *Why Mosquitoes Buzz in People's Ears,* and dozens of other titles. Many of her stories are about Africa. Her books appear in many languages and are read in many countries.

Spencer Abraham

Abraham, Spencer (b. 1953), politician. Abraham, from East Lansing, serves as secretary of energy for President George W. Bush. Abraham served as U.S. senator from Michigan from 1995 to 2001 and was the only Arab-American in the **Senate.** He was chairman of Michigan's Republican Party from 1991 to 1993 before winning his senate seat. His grandparents came to the United States from Lebanon, a Middle-Eastern country, and while Abraham was a senator, he worked on the immigration committee to help others come to the United States.

Daniels, Jeff (b. 1955), entertainer. As an actor, director, writer, and producer, Daniels has entertained audiences as a goofy comedian, villian, hero, and hometown legend in his performances both on the screen and the stage. Raised in Chelsea, Daniels founded the Purple Rose Theater Company there and produced several plays he wrote himself. His 2001 film *Escanaba in Da Moonlight* was written about hunting season in Michigan's Upper Peninsula.

Dewey, Thomas E. (1902–1971), politician. Dewey was born in Owosso, Michigan, and graduated from the University of Michigan in 1923. After earning his law degree in 1926, he was elected New York's **attorney general** and worked to stop crime, especially illegal gambling. He served as governor of New York for three terms (1942–1955). He unsuccessfully ran for U.S. president against Franklin D. Roosevelt in 1944.

Edmonds, Sarah Emma (1842–1898), soldier. Edmonds was one of about 400 women who fought in the Civil War (1861–1865). In order to join with men from Flint, where she lived, she disguised herself and used the name Frank Thompson. After several tries, she was sworn in and left for Virginia. Not only was she able to keep up her disguise while with the Northern troops, but she became a spy and entered **Confederate** camps dressed differently, depending upon her mission. Once she pretended to be a slave called "Cuff." Another time she dressed up as an Irish peddler-woman as she went behind enemy lines. Her adventures finally ended when she became sick with **malaria.** The army thought she was a **deserter,** but years later, she was awarded an **honorable discharge** from the army.

Sarah Emma Edmonds

Gerald Ford

Ford, Gerald R. Jr. (b. 1913), politician. Ford moved to Grand Rapids from Nebraska as a young boy. His birth name was Lesley Lynch King Jr. His mother and father divorced and he was renamed when his mother married his stepfather, Gerald R. Ford. After graduating from the University of Michigan in 1935, he could have played professional football for the Detroit Lions or the Green Bay Packers, but he decided on coaching and law school. Ford graduated from Yale Law School in 1941, then returned to Grand Rapids to practice law. He joined the navy during World War II (1939–1945), earned ten battle stars during his tour of duty, and rose to the rank of lieutenant commander.

Ford became interested in politics and won a seat in the United States House of Representatives. He became the only U.S. president from Michigan when he took office in 1974. He holds the record for being the only non-elected vice president and president. He became the vice president during Richard Nixon's administration when Vice President Spiro Agnew **resigned.** When President Nixon was forced to resign from office, Vice President Ford became the president. He was awarded the Medal of Freedom for the way he led the country after the Watergate scandal and during the Vietnam War.

Franklin, Aretha (b. 1942), singer. Franklin began her singing career in the church choir. Her father was the church's reverend, and her mother was a gospel singer. Franklin started recording albums when she was just fourteen. Since then, she has had twenty number-one rhythm-and-blues hits and has won seventeen Grammys as well as a Grammy Lifetime Achievement Award. Franklin is often called the Queen of Soul, and her voice was once declared a Michigan natural resource.

Gordy, Berry Jr. (b. 1929), businessperson. In 1959 Gordy formed a company in Detroit called Motown Records. He wrote songs and recorded rhythm-and-blues songs in his house. The Motown Sound became popular in the 1960s and 1970s. He helped launch the careers of local musical acts such as Diana Ross and the Supremes, Stevie Wonder, Smokey Robinson and the Miracles, Mary Wells, Gladys Knight and the Pips, the Jackson Five, Marvin Gaye, the Four Tops, and the Temptations. Gordy sold Motown Records in 1988.

Aretha Franklin

Harwell, Ernie (b. 1918), sports announcer. With his legendary "Long gone!" announcement as a home run sailed out of Comerica Park, Harwell was the voice of Detroit Tigers baseball for 43 years. He began broadcasting the minor league Atlanta Crackers in 1946 and moved up to the major leagues in 1948 with the Brooklyn Dodgers before coming to Detroit. During his career with the Tigers, Harwell was well-loved by both the players and the fans. He is a member of the National Baseball Hall of Fame and the National Sportscasters Hall of Fame.

Johnson, Earvin "Magic" (b. 1959), athlete. Magic Johnson is a well-known name to basketball fans. While

Magic attended Everett High School in Lansing, he set records and was picked for the All-State basketball team all four years. He got his nickname, Magic, during his sophomore year of college. At Michigan State University, he helped his team win the National Collegiate Athletic Association (N.C.A.A.) national title in 1979. Johnson was the first player chosen in the 1979 NBA draft. He became a Los Angeles Laker and had many successful years on the court. He shocked basketball fans when he retired in 1991, announcing that he had been diagnosed with HIV, the virus that causes AIDS. He came back to the Lakers in 1996 and played one more year before he retired again. He now is a co-owner of the Lakers, speaks to teens about AIDS, and supports other worthy causes.

Earvin "Magic" Johnson

Keck, Donald B. (b. 1941) inventor. Keck was born in Lansing and graduated from Michigan State University three times—when he earned his bachelors, masters, and doctorate degrees. Keck and two other researchers at Corning Glass invented **fiber optics,** allowing computers to receive and transmit high-speed connections on the Internet "information highway."

Donald B. Keck

Kellogg, William K. (1860–1951), inventor. Kellogg invented his famous breakfast cereal while helping his brother, Dr. John Harvey Kellogg. They were trying to invent a breakfast food for Dr. Kellogg's patients, and the cereal recipe for Corn Flakes came about when Will accidentally let the mixture sit too long before rolling it out. The crisp, dry cereal flakes were popular with patients. One of the patients, **Charles W. Post,** had come to Battle Creek for treatment, but when he tasted the multigrain cereal, he stayed there and went into production for himself.

William K. Kellogg

Kendrick, Pearl (1890–1980), scientist. Kendrick lived much of her adult life in Grand Rapids, working in public health. Dr. Kendrick developed the DPT **vaccine** to protect people for **diptheria, pertussis,** and **tetanus.** Before 1939, these three diseases were life threatening.

Lewis, Joe (1914–1981), athlete. Lewis's family moved north to Michigan from Alabama during the **Great Migration.** Lewis was poor, large for his age, had speech problems, and did not do well in school. However, Joe was accepting of others and generous. He began boxing in his neighborhood and practiced to become an amateur boxer. In 1935 Lewis boxed at Madison Square Garden and won his match. He represented the United States at the 1936 Summer Olympics in Berlin, Germany. He became the world's heavy-weight boxing champion in 1937. The Joe Lewis Arena in downtown Detroit is named in his honor.

Joe Lewis

Charles Lindbergh

Lindbergh, Charles (1902–1974), **aviator.** Lindbergh's life began in Detroit in 1902—before cars were popular and before the first successful airplane flight. Twenty-five years later, he made world history. He was the first aviator to make a solo, nonstop flight across the Atlantic Ocean. For this reason, he was called the Lone Eagle. The flight in the *Spirit of St. Louis* lasted 33.5 hours. Today, nonstop flights between New York City and Paris last less than eight hours.

Madonna (b. 1958), entertainer. Born in Bay City, Madonna Louise Veronica Ciccone became an international music star. She won a scholarship to study dance at the University of Michigan, but she left for New York City before graduating. Along with hit records, albums, and world tours, Madonna has performed in movies and on stage on both Broadway and in London.

Malcolm X

Malcolm X (1925–1965), **activist.** Born in Nebraska in 1925, Malcolm Little grew up in Lansing, Michigan. As an adult, he changed his name to Malcolm X. He spoke out for the rights of African Americans and tried to help them be unified. He was known for his association first with the Nation of Islam, sometimes known as the Black Muslims, and later with the Organization of Afro-American Unity, which he founded after breaking with the Nation of Islam. On February 21, 1965, he was shot and killed. Three members of the Nation of Islam were convicted of the murder.

Milliken, William G. (b. 1922), politician. Milliken was born in Traverse City. He served in the Michigan state **senate** and one term as **lieutenant governor** before he took the governor's post. As governor of Michigan, Milliken served longer than any other governor did—from 1969 to 1982.

Parks, Rosa (b. 1913), activist. By refusing to give up her bus seat to a white man in the **segregated** South, Parks sparked the United States **civil rights movement** and became a symbol of the power of nonviolent protest. As a result of Parks' actions, Dr. Martin Luther King Jr. led a **boycott** of the bus company that lasted more than a year until the city government agreed to start nonsegregated busing. Parks moved to Detroit in 1957. In honor of her work, the first Monday following February 4 is Mrs. Rosa Parks' Day in the state of Michigan.

Parsons, John T. (b. 1913), inventor. Parsons was born in Detroit in 1913. He earned the title Father of the Second Industrial Revolution with his invention of numerical control. His idea makes machinery operate accurately with the help of computers. His system is used in building everything from huge airplanes to tiny computer chips. He also invented the huge fuel lines used in rocket boosters that send astronauts into space.

Radner, Gilda (1946–1989), entertainer. Radner knew she wanted to perform from an early age. She met famous guests who stayed at her father's hotel in Detroit. She performed in movies and plays but is best known for her roles on *Saturday Night Live*. When Radner was diagnosed with cancer, she formed a support group called Gilda's Club. Her husband, comedian Gene Wilder, expanded on her idea and created an ovarian cancer research center in her memory. Michigan has several Gilda's Clubs, which are support groups for cancer patients and their families and friends. There are many other Gilda's Clubs throughout the nation.

Della Reese

Reese, Della (b. 1932), entertainer. An actor, singer, talk show host, and author, Reese first started singing in church in her hometown of Detroit when she was six years old. By the age of thirteen, she was touring, and at eighteen became the first performer to bring gospel music to the casinos of Las Vegas. She appeared many times on several television series and played the role of Tess on the television series *Touched By An Angel.* This role earned her both Emmy Award and Golden Globe nominations. Also, this role earned Reese the National Association for the Advancement of Colored People (NAACP) Image Award for Outstanding Lead Actress in a Television Drama Series six years in a row.

Robinson, Sugar Ray (1921–1989), athlete. Robinson was a famous boxer from Detroit. His real name was Walker Smith Jr., but he used the name Robinson. Fans started calling him Sugar Ray after a reporter said he was "sweet as sugar." Robinson's career as a boxer included a record of 174 wins, 19 defeats, and 6 ties.

The Supremes: Florence Ballard, Diana Ross (center), and Mary Wilson.

Ross, Diana (b. 1944), singer. As lead singer with the Supremes, Ross's group became the most popular female musical group in the 1960s. During this time, the Supremes had twelve number-one singles and three number-one albums. They were second only to the Beatles in record sales in that decade. The group changed names to Diana Ross and the Supremes before Ross broke away from the group entirely and began recording on her own. As a solo artist, six of Ross's singles hit number one. In 1988, Diana Ross and the Supremes were inducted into the Rock and Roll Hall of Fame.

Saarinen, Eliel (1850–1973) and **Eero** (1910–1961), architects. Eliel and his son Eero came to Detroit from Finland in 1923. They designed famous buildings in the

United States and several in Michigan. They created the General Motors Technical Center in Warren and the Gateway Arch in St. Louis.

Seger, Bob (b. 1945), entertainer. Born in Dearborn, Seger has lived in Michigan all his life. He has been a performer for over 30 years and is best known for his songs "Old Time Rock 'n' Roll," "Shakedown," "Night Moves," and "Like a Rock."

Sheehan, John C. (1915–1992), inventor. Sheehan was born in Battle Creek and received more than 40 **patents** for his inventions. One of his most important achievements was discovering the chemical formula of the **antibiotic** penicillin. Before his research, it took months to produce a very small amount of the natural form of this lifesaving drug.

Michigan Astronauts

Since the early days of flight, Michigan has produced eleven astronauts. Alfred Worden (b. 1932) came from Jackson. In 1971 he orbited the moon with Apollo 15. He orbited the moon three times and took remote-controlled pictures of the moon's surface. Then he took a space walk to collect film that was in the cameras on the outside of his command ship. You can learn more about him and these other Michigan astronauts at the Michigan Space and Science Center in Astronaut Worden's hometown of Jackson: **Michael Bloomfield, Roger B. Chaffee, Gregory Jarvis, Brent Jett Jr., David Leestma, Jerry Linenger, Richard Searfoss, Donald McMonagle, and Brewster Shaw Jr.**

Lily Tomlin

Thomas, Margaret (b. 1938), entertainer. Better known as Marlo Thomas, she performed on *That Girl*, a television program in the 1960s. She was born in Deerfield, but her father, **Danny Thomas** (1914–1991), worked in Hollywood. Marlo and her siblings were raised in Hollywood, where Danny worked. Marlo won awards for her television performances and so did her father. Danny was also the founder of St. Jude Children's Research Hospital. Marlo still works to support her father's hospital.

Tomlin, Lily (b. 1939), entertainer. Tomlin comes from Detroit. She has acted in movies, on television shows, and on Broadway and has won many awards during her career. She created many funny characters for herself, especially while she performed on the television show *Laugh In* from 1969 to 1974.

Van Allsburg, Chris (b. 1949), writer, sculptor. Van Allsburg was born in East Grand Rapids and graduated from the University of Michigan and the Rhode Island School of Design. *The Polar Express* is one of his award-winning books. Another of his award-winning books is *Jumanji,* which also became a movie.

Wonder, Stevie (b. 1950), singer. Wonder was born in Saginaw as Steveland Judkins. Blind since birth, he hit the music scene at age 11, playing drums, harmonica, and piano. He became known as "Little Stevie Wonder" and was a large part of the Motown sound during the 1960s and 1970s. His musical career includes 17 Grammys and an Academy Award. He has sold over 70 million albums.

Stevie Wonder

Map of Michigan

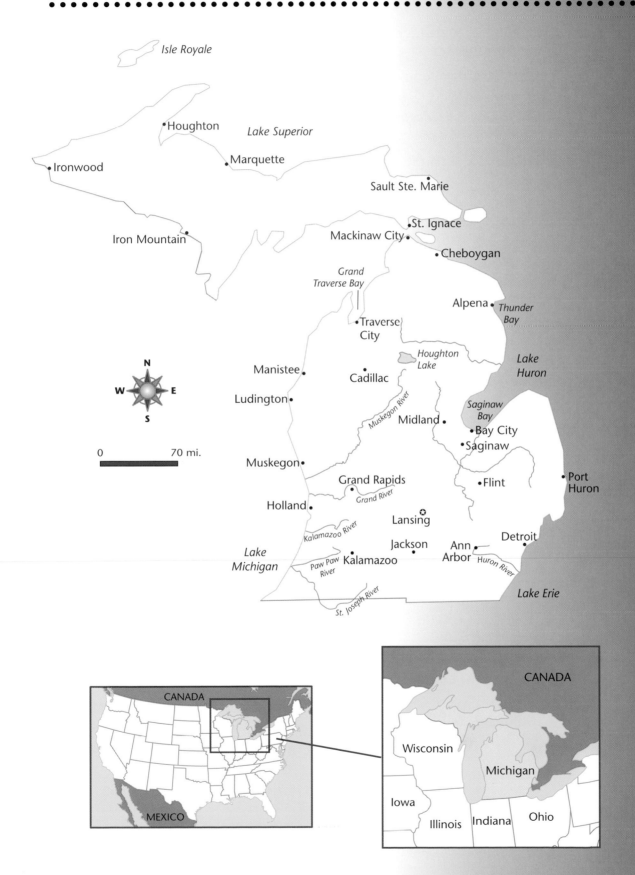

Isle Royale

•Houghton   Lake Superior

•Ironwood   •Marquette

Sault Ste. Marie

•St. Ignace
Mackinaw City•

Iron Mountain   •Cheboygan

Grand
Traverse Bay

Alpena•   Thunder
Bay

•Traverse
City

Houghton
Lake   Lake
Huron

Manistee•   Cadillac•

Ludington•

Saginaw
Bay

Muskegon River

Midland•   •Bay City
•Saginaw

0   70 mi.

Muskegon•

Grand Rapids•   •Flint   •Port
Huron

Grand River

Holland•   Lansing

Kalamazoo River   Detroit•

Jackson•   Ann
Arbor•

Lake
Michigan   Paw Paw
River   Kalamazoo•   Huron River

St. Joseph River   Lake Erie

CANADA

CANADA

Wisconsin   Michigan

Iowa

MEXICO   Illinois   Indiana   Ohio

Glossary

activist someone who publicly supports a cause

agricultural having to do with farming

allies groups or individuals united for a common purpose

ambitious desiring power and success

antibiotic substance produced by living things that is used to kill or prevent the growth of harmful germs

archaeologist person who studies history through the things that people have made or built

artifact something created by humans for a practical purpose during a certain time period

attorney general chief law officer of a nation or state

authentic being what it really seems to be

aviator someone who flies aircraft

baron person who has great influence in some field of activity

boycott to refuse to have dealings with someone or buy a certain product until a demand is met

canal human-made waterway for boats

cholera infection that affects the digestive system

civil rights movement demand for equal rights for African Americans

Confederate word used to refer to one of the eleven Southern states that broke away from the United States in 1860 and 1861

culture ideas, skills, arts, and a way of life of a certain people at a certain time

descent to be born of

deserter someone who leaves the military without permission

diptheria disease that affects a person's breathing

diverse having variety

ethnic belonging to a group with a particular culture

famine time when food is scarce and people are starving

fertile bearing crops or vegetation in abundance

fiber optics thin transparent fibers of glass or plastic that transmit light

fort strong building used for defense against enemy attack

Great Depression period of economic hardship that began in 1929, in which unemployment was high and many businesses failed

Great Migration movement of thousands of African Americans from Southern states to Northern states

heritage something that comes from one's ancestors

honorable discharge release from the armed forces with a good record

humanitarian devoted to and working for the health and happiness of other people

immigrant person moving to another country to settle

industry group of businesses that offers a similar product or service

interchangable able to be put into the place of another

Jesuit member of the Roman Catholic Society of Jesus who is devoted to missionary work

lieutenant governor second-in-command of a state, after the governor

locks enclosures with gates at each end used in raising and lowering boats as they pass from level to level

malaria disease spread by the bite of a mosquito

mammoth prehistoric relative of today's elephant

mastodon prehistoric relative of today's elephant

migrate to move from one place to another

mission group that sets forth on a task, particularly to spread certain religious views

occupation one's business or profession

patent protected by a document that gives the inventor of something the only right to make, use, and sell the invention for a certain number of years

pertussis disease that causes coughing and difficulty breathing

plague deadly illness

prehistoric from the time before history was written

prosperous makes money

quadricycle Henry Ford's first experimental vehicle. It ran on four bicycle tires.

resign formally giving up an office

rural having to do with the country or farmland

schooner ship usually having two masts, used for transporting goods and passengers

segregate to set one type of people apart from others

senate upper and smaller branch of a legislature in a country or state

sesquicentennial 150-year anniversary

strait narrow channel connecting two bodies of water

suburban having to do with a city or town just outside a larger city

telecommute work at home through an electronic connection to an office

tetanus disease that causes muscle spasms

urban having to do with the city

vaccine material used to protect against disease

More Books to Read

Barenblat, Rachel and Jean Craven. *Michigan the Wolverine State*. Cleveland: World Almanac Education, 2002.

Brill, Marlene Targ. *Michigan*. Tarrytown, N.Y.: Benchmark Books, 1998.

Heinrichs, Anne. *Michigan*. Minneapolis: Compass Point Books, 2003.

Hintz, Martin and R. Conrad Stein. *Michigan*. Danbury, Conn.: Children's Press, 1998.

Johnson, Elizabeth M. *Michigan*. Danbury, Conn.: Children's Press, 2002.

Index

About the Author

Award-winning photographer and journalist Marcia Schonberg is the author of travel guides, nonfiction children's books, and the Heinemann Library Ohio State Studies books. She has contributed to *Michigan Living* and writes regularly for daily newspapers and regional and national magazines. A mother of three, Marcia resides in the Midwest with her husband Bill and golden retriever, Cassie.